If you carry your childhood with you, you never become older...

First published in Great Britain in 2007 by BaileyHart Publishing.
BHP House, 8 Oman Avenue, London NW2 6BG

Copyright BaileyHart Publishing 2007
Text and knitting design copyright Fiona Bailey 2007

The right of Fiona Bailey to be identified as the author of this
work has been asserted by her in accordance with the
Copyright, Designs and Patents Act, 1988.

A CIP catalogue record for this book is
available from the British Library.

10 9 8 7 6 5 4 3 2 1
ISBN : 978-0-9552843-1-1

Book design by: SG Design
Photographer: Richard Bailey

Paper used is natural recyclable made from
wood grown in sustainable forests.

Printed and bound in Hong Kong.

simply knit...

hats

fiona bailey

photographs by richard bailey

We do not remember days;
we remember moments

contents...

introduction…

If you are new to knitting it can sometimes be quite daunting to take on a big project, which is why my designs have been kept very simple. The simplest really can be done in a few hours, even whilst watching the television, so will never be left half finished. When they are completed though, they look absolutely fabulous and if knitted for a gift, your friends will think that you are a genius. There is nothing better than knitting for a baby or small child, to create something so small is a real pleasure and to then give this to a friend or relative's new baby is a really special gift.

I have shown a few ways to wrap the hats at the back of the book and I know from experience this will create a lasting impression that you are by far their cleverest and loveliest friend!

I do have to make a confession though, compared to many authors of other knitting books on the market I am a complete beginner. I am not internationally renowned, nor have I studied for years at textile college. I started knitting as a teenager, but only picked up my needles again a relatively short time ago, (when friends and relatives started having babies) and became hooked on producing small knitted gifts. This is why I have written this book, to show that even beginners can create wonderful items of knitwear for their family and friends, whilst enjoying this wonderfully rewarding pastime.

As a mother of three young children and eleven nephews and nieces I have had lots of practise in thinking about what to give for a birth present or birthday presents. I wanted to steer away from the tradition of pale blue for baby boys and pale pink or yellow for the girls. The colourways I have chosen for these designs are for the modern baby and child, the young dudes and dudesses who will be surfing, skiing and skate boarding before we know it.

This is a book for beginners to start and improve their knitting skills and is an excellent way for new or young knitters to gain confidence, to go on and tackle bigger projects.

techniques...

As this is a book primarily for beginners, I have used only the simplest techniques in knitting, but to the maximum effect. Although I have specified which yarns and colour ways to use, don't be afraid to experiment with other wools and different colours. The fun in knitting can be discovering different yarns and working out which colours you think complement each other.

Knitting is only made up of two stitches – 'knit' and 'purl'. Once you have mastered these two stitches, other more complicated designs will be within your reach.

Opposite you will see photographic illustrations of the three stitches used to make up all of the patterns in this book, all created using knit and purl.

1 Garter stitch is simply when you knit every row. This really is the beginners stitch and can be used to make many items, from scarves and hats to jumpers.

2 Stocking stitch is created when you knit one row and purl the other. It is widely used on anything from socks and slippers to jumpers and shawls.

3 Rib stitch is when you combine knit and purl alternately along one row. This sequence of stitches is commonly used on collars and cuffs.

casting on

The first thing to do, before you can start knitting is 'to cast on'.

This means to make loops or 'stitches' with a length of yarn onto one of the knitting needles. There are a few ways of doing this, but I have illustrated one of the easiest ways here. Like anything new, a little practise makes perfect and before long it will become second nature to you.

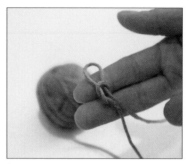

1 Make a loop knot ensuring that you leave enough yarn for the amount of stitches needed.

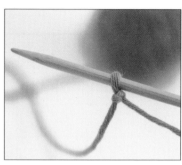

2 Insert needle into the loop.

3 Take the ball end of the yarn and wrap over your left thumb.

4 With the needle in your right hand insert it into the loop under your left thumb as shown.

5 Take the loose end of the yarn and wrap under the needle and place between needle and thumb.

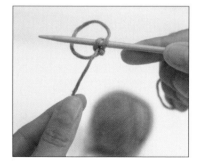

6 Take the yarn on the thumb and push the loop over the needle and then pull ball end of yarn loosely.

Continue casting on until you reach the number of stitches in your pattern.

knit and purl

Knit stitch

To begin your first row of knitting you must first cast on the appropriate number of stitches that the pattern asks you to. The knit stitch is really just a simple four-step process, which I have illustrated here. Once you have completed the four steps you will have transferred all the stitches on the left hand needle onto the right hand needle. You then transfer the needle holding the finished stitches into your left hand and begin the process again with another row of knit stitches, to create a fabric known as the 'garter stitch', which you can see in the illustration on page 11.

Purl stitch

The purl stitch and the knit stitch are quite similar in the way that you work them, the only difference being that with the purl stitch you hold the yarn at the front of your work instead of at the back. Once you have mastered knit and purl, you will have mastered knitting! Well, as with everything, practise makes perfect, but with knit and purl you are ready to combine them to create all sorts of different fabrics. For instance, by working one row knit and one row purl alternately you will have made stocking stitch as shown on page 11.

1 Place the point of the right hand needle into the stitch on the left hand needle as shown.

2 Holding the yarn in the right hand, wrap it over the point of the right hand needle to make a loop.

3 Pull the new loop on the right hand needle under and through the loop on the left hand needle.

4 Slide the stitch off the point of the left hand needle. You have now knitted a stitch on your right hand needle.

1 Place the point of the right hand needle into the stitch on the left hand needle as shown.

2 Whilst holding the yarn in your right hand, wrap the yarn over the point of the right hand needle to make a loop.

3 Pull the new loop on the right hand needle under and through the loop on the left hand needle.

4 Now slide the stitch off the point of the left hand needle, which will leave a new 'purled' stitch on the right needle.

casting off

To stop your finished piece of knitting from unravelling we do something called 'casting off' the stitches.

This is the process of taking one stitch loop through the next all along the length of the needle as you knit across the row.

Sometimes the instructions for a design will simply say 'cast off x amount of stitches', which means you should knit each stitch as you cast off.

In other cases it will tell you to 'cast off x amount of stitches in a pattern', in this case you should knit or purl each stitch in the pattern and cast off the required amount of stitches.

1 To cast off, knit two stitches onto the right hand needle.

2 Insert the left hand needle into the first stitch on the right hand needle.

3 Lift the first stitch on the right hand needle over the second stitch on the right hand needle.

4 Take the left hand needle from the stitch leaving one stitch on the right hand needle.

5 Repeat this action on all remaining stitches across the row, until one stitch remains.

6 To finish casting off, cut the yarn and thread it through the last stitch and pull to tighten.

adding a contrasting colour

In several patterns in this book you are required to change the colour of wool. Don't be daunted by this as the process really is very simple, whether you are knitting stripes or following a grid, changing colour at the start of a row, or in the middle.

1 Place your right hand needle into the first stitch of the row.

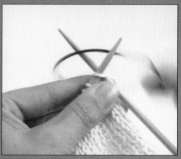

2 Holding the contrasting yarn in your right hand, wrap it over the point of the right hand needle to make a loop.

3 Pull the new loop in the contrasting colour through the first loop on the left hand needle.

4 Slide the stitch off the point of the left hand needle. You now have one stitch in your contrasting colour

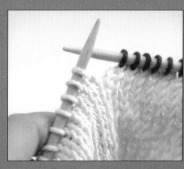

5 Continue knitting across the row with the contrasting colour.

6 Once you have knitted a few rows you can see the stripe clearly. Once you have finished ensure that you secure and sew in the loose yarn.

increasing

Adding or taking away stitches from a row will give form and shape to your knitting.

This is called 'increasing' and 'decreasing' and is used to shape most of the hats in this book, so will be something you need to practise. There are other ways, but this way will stand you in good stead for now.

1 To 'increase' by 'casting on', insert the right hand needle into the first stitch and pull a loop through.

2 This time, do not drop the stitch from the left needle, but insert the left needle into the new loop and slip it off the right needle.

3 You will now have an extra stitch on the left hand needle. Begin the next row in the usual way.

decreasing

Again you will need to practise 'decreasing' as this will be in a number of the patterns in this book.

The simplest way of decreasing is by knitting two stitches together as shown.

1 Place the right hand needle into two stitches (through front or back loops) and then wrap the yarn over the needle.

2 With the two stitches still on the left hand needle, pull the yarn under and through both stitches at the same time.

3 Now you can drop the two stitches from the left hand needle and you will have just made two stitches into one.

patterns...

From traditional pom pom hats, to simple but funky square hats, a beautifully warm scarf hat through to a cool in the summer denim sun hat.

I have tried to create a range of hats that will suit all ages and 'style' of child. Some children will love the camouflage hat as they run off into the woods, whilst the skull and cross-bone hat will be a sure-fire winner, whilst combing the beach on a blustery day.

The flower hat reminds me of the 1920's flapper hats that young ladies would wear, whilst the beret is an old time favourite. All the designs have a contemporary twist to them, whilst the colour ways I have chosen are not the traditional pastel blues and yellows usually associated with knitting for babies but are bold, confident and definitely make a statement.

The main idea for this book was to make everything easy, hence the title easy knits. With this in mind I have kept the pattern instructions as simple as possible, without any confusing abbreviations and in the simplest of language.

I'm hoping that you will be able to work on these hats when you get a quiet moment and find them easy enough to finish within your busy schedule. They are also useful for youngsters to start the 'call of knitting' on.

skull and crossbone hat

Of all the hats in the book this one is perhaps the hardest, as you have the skull and crossbone motif to knit. Don't be put off though, as it isn't as hard as it looks.

I have used Rowan 4 ply cotton, which feels really smooth to the touch, as well as being naturally warm. It might look like this is one for the boys, but the girls enjoy this hat as well. If you're still unsure, why not try using pink or red for the skull and crossbone design. If there are a few children in your family or the family you are knitting for, why not choose different colours for the motif to match each child.

Think of days by the seaside in blustery weather holding your arms out as wide as they can go and leaning into the wind.

Sizes
6-12 months, (12-24 months, 24-36 months).

Materials
Rowan 4 ply cotton.
All sizes require 50 grams, with small quantity of contrasting cotton for skull pattern.
3mm needles.

Tension
10cm + 10cm square should have 27 stitches and 37 rows.

Method
Cast on 99 (111,123) stitches in main colour.
Using stocking-stitch work 10 (12,12) rows.

Work 40 rows using the chart with 38 (44,50) stitches either side.
Work 2 rows stocking-stitch.

Shape crown
Knit 6 (knit 3 together, knit 9) 7 (8,9) times. Knit 3 together, knit 6.
Purl 1 row.
Knit 5 (knit 3 together, knit 7) 7 (8,9) times. Knit 3 together, knit 5.
Purl 1 row.
Knit 4 (knit 3 together, knit 3) 7 (8,9) times. Knit 3 together, knit 4.
Purl 1 row.
Knit 3 (knit 3 together, knit 3) 7 (8,9) times. Knit 3 together, knit 3.
Purl 1 row.
Knit 2 (knit 2 together, knit 1) 7 (8,9) times. Knit 3 together, knit 2.
Purl 1 row.
Knit 2 together to last stitch. Knit 1.
Stocking-stitch 9 rows. Thread wool through remaining stitches, draw tight and join seam.

rows

To create the motif of skull and crossbones on this hat you will need to follow the chart opposite. The chart represents 23 stitches across and 40 rows. You will need to read the pattern carefully and knit the correct number of stitches either side of the chart, once you get going it will become simpler.

As you can see you will need to add a contrasting colour. This is also a simple process, have a look on page 15 which will explain how this is done.

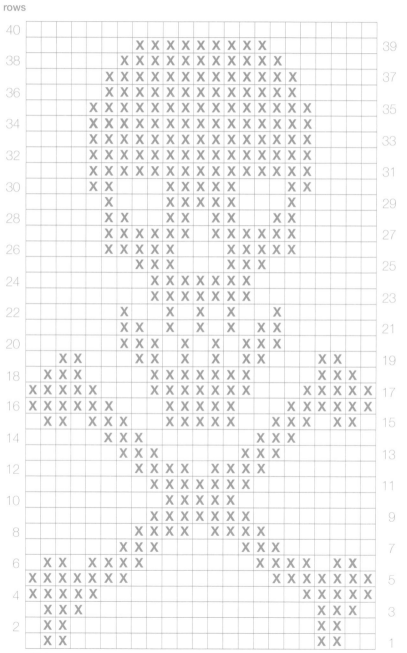

stitches

flower hat

The flower hat reminds me of the kind of hat that ladies in the 1920's would wear. If you have seen the children's film Bugsy Malone you will know what I mean.

Even without the flower there is a warmth and femininity to this hat, which the adding of the flower only enhances.

This hat involves the use of stocking stitch (see page 23) I have used merino yarn for this item, although you can just as easily try using cotton. The deep red and purple work very well together creating a subtle but distinct look.

Hat

Sizes
6-12 months, (12-24 months, 24-36 months).

Materials
Jaeger Matchmaker merino DK.
All sizes require 50 grams, with a small amount of contrasting wool for stripe and flower decoration. 4mm needles.

Tension
10cm + 10cm square should have 19 stitches and 27 rows.

Method
Cast on 130 (146,162) stitches.
Using stocking-stitch work 6 rows.
Knit 2 together along length of row.
65 (73, 81) stitches.
Purl 1 row.
With right side facing, change to contrasting colour and knit 1 row.

Starting with a knit row, work 5 rows in reverse stocking-stitch ending with a wrong side row.
Break off contrasting colour and return to main colour.

Starting with a knit row, continue in stocking-stitch until work measures 11 (12,13) cms from beginning of contrasting colour band, end with a wrong-side row.

Shape top.
Large size only:
Row 1 (right side): Knit 8, knit 2 together 8 times, knit 1. (73 stitches).
Purl 1 row.
Medium and large size only:
Next row (right side): (Knit 7, knit 2 together) 8 times, knit 1. (65 stitches).
All sizes:
Next row (right side) (Knit 6, knit 2 together) 8 times. knit 1. (57 stitches).
Purl 1 row.
(Knit 5, knit 2 together) 8 times. Knit 1. (49 stitches).
Purl 1 row.
(Knit 4, knit 2 together) 8 times. Knit 1. (41 stitches).
Purl 1 row.
(Knit 3, knit 2 together) 8 times. Knit 1. (33 stitches).
Purl 1 row.
(Knit 2, knit 2 together) 8 times. Knit 1. (25 stitches).
Purl 1 row.
(Knit 1, knit 2 together) 8 times. Knit 1. (17 stitches).
Purl 1 row.
(Knit 2 together) 8 times. Knit 1. (9 stitches).
Purl 1 row.
Break wool and thread through remaining 9 stitches.
Pull tight and fasten off .
Join side seam using a large sewing needle and matching thread.

Flower

Using main colour wool, cast on 30 stitches.
Working in stocking-stitch knit 8 rows.
Next row knit 2 together across the row (15 stitches).
Purl 1 row. Break off wool and thread through remaining stitches, pull tight and fasten securely.
Sew together the end seams to form a circle.
Make another flower using the contrasting colour, but curl this inside the main colour circle to form flower centre. Attach both to the hat above the contrasting band of colour.

beret

Who doesn't love the beret? Worn by revolutionaries from Che Guevara and Citizen Smith right through to Mary Quant. (Who would have thought you would have heard those three in the same sentence.)

The beret synonymous with the French, is here knitted using matchmaker merino 4 ply yarn, to give a lovely softness and warmth. I have also added a subtly contrasting colour as a stripe at the base of the hat. Again experiment using different colours; pink berets always look fantastic on young girls, whilst my daughter has a pale green one with an orange trim that she adores.

Sizes
6-12 months, (12-24 months, 24-36 months).

Materials
Jaeger matchmaker merino 4ply.
All sizes require 50 grams with a small amount of contrast wool for stripe.
1 pair of 2.75mm kniting needles.
1 pair of 3mm knitting needles.

Tension
10cm + 10cm square should have 33 stitches and 37 rows.

Method
Using 2.75mm needles and the contrasting colour cast on 124 (136,144) stitches.
Change to main colour and work 8 (10,10) rows in knit 1, purl 1 rib.

Change to 3mm needles.
(Knit 1, increase 1) repeat to end of row. 186 (204,216) stitches.
Working in stocking-stitch starting with a purl row work 19 (23,27) rows.

(Knit 2 stitches together, knit 4) to end of row. 155 (170,180) stitches.
Work 5 (7,9) rows.
(Knit 2 stitches together, knit 3) to end of row. 124 (136,144) stitches.
Work 3 (5,7) rows.
(Knit 2 stitches together, knit 2) repeat to end of row. 93 (102,108) stitches.
Work 1 (3,5) rows.
(Knit 2 stitches together, knit 1) repeat to end of row. 62 (68,72) stitches.
Work 1 row.
(Knit 2 stitches together, knit 4).
1st and 2nd sizes only until last 2 stitches, knit 2.
3rd size keep knitting and decreasing to end of row. 52 (57,60) stitches.
Work 1 row.
(Knit 2 stitches together, knit 3).
1st and 2nd sizes until last 2 stitches, knit 2.
3rd size knit to the end of row. 42 (46,48) stitches.
Work 1 row.
(Knit 2 together, knit 2).
1st and 2nd sizes until last 2 stitches, knit 2.
3rd size knit to end of the row. 32 (35,36) stitches. Work 1 row.
(Knit 2 together, knit 1).
1st and 2nd sizes until last 2 stitches, knit 2.
3rd size knit to end of the row. 22 (24,24) stitches.
Purl 2 together across remaining stitches, draw up tightly and fasten off securely.
Join side seam.

beanie hat

The beanie hat is an all time favourite for babies. This was one of the first hats that I ever knitted, because it was so simple. The stocking stitch and shaping are easy to work and there is a simple roll edged brim, which allows you to adjust the size to fit the baby's head.

I have used Debbie Bliss cotton cashmere for this hat, which is ideal for newborns because it is so soft to the touch. I haven't though gone for soft colours. The usual pale blues and pale yellows have been thrown out in favour of oranges and greens, not bright and garish, but bold enough to make a statement. This hat makes a wonderful gift for the newborn baby, especially when packaged nicely.

Sizes
Newborn, (6-18 months,18-24 months).

Materials
Debbie Bliss cotton cashmere DK.
All sizes require 50 grams with 10 grams of contrast colour for rim.
4 mm knitting needles.

Tension
10cm + 10cm square should have 27 stitches and 20 rows.

Method
Cast on 81 (89,97) stitches in contrasting colour Knit 8 rows in stocking stitch.
Change to main colour and work 16 (18,20) rows in stocking stitch).

Shape Crown
Knit 1, knit 2 stitches together, knit 8 (9,10) stitches. Repeat to end of row. 73 (81,89).

Newborn size – purl 1 row.

Medium and large sizes – work 3 rows in stocking stitch.
Knit 1, knit 2 stitches together, knit 7, (8,9) stitches. Repeat to end of row. 65 (73,81).

Newborn and medium only – Purl 1 row.

Large size – Work 3 rows in stocking stitch

Knit 1, knit 2 stitches together, knit 6 (7,8) stitches. Repeat to end of row. 57 (65,73).
Purl 1 row.
Knit 1, knit 2 stitches together, knit 5 (6,7) stitches. Repeat to end of row. 49 (57,65).
Purl 1 row.
Knit 1, knit 2 stitches together, knit 4 (5,6) stitches. Repeat to end of row. 41 (47,57).
Purl 1 row.
Knit 1, knit 2 stitches together, knit 3 (4,5) stitches. Repeat to end of row.33 (41,49).
Purl 1 row.
Knit 1, knit 2 stitches together, knit 2 (3,4) stitches. Repeat to end of row. 25 (33,41).
Purl 1 row.
Knit 1, knit 2 stitches together, knit 1 (2,3) stitches. Repeat to end of row. 17 (25,33).
Purl 1 row.

Newborn size only – Knit 1, knit 2 stitches together 8 times. 9 stitches.
Thread yarn through remaining stitches, pull tight and fasten off.

Medium and large sizes – Knit 1, knit 2 stitches together, knit 0 (1,2). Repeat to end of row. (17,25)
Purl 1 row.

Medium size only – Knit 1, knit 2 stitches together 8 times. 9 stitches.
Thread yarn through remaining stitches, pull tight and fasten off.

Large size only – Knit 1, knit 2 stitches together, knit 0 (0,1). Repeat to end of row. 17 stitches.
Purl one row.
Knit 1, knit 2 stitches together 8 times. 9 stitches.
Purl one row.
Thread yarn through remaining stitches, pull tight and fasten off.

Scarf

Using 4 mm needles cast on 25 stitches and work 12 rows in plain knit (garter stitch) in each colour until length required.
Cast off.

There is a garden in every childhood, an enchanted place where colours are brighter, the air softer, and the morning more fragrant than ever again

camouflage hat

Here we have a hat that brings us right up to date. Every young boy seems to have at least some piece of camouflage clothing in his wardrobe and this clever little hat is a welcome addition. I have added earflaps for extra warmth and that military feel.

The wool is 100% hand spun Chunky Debbie Bliss Maya, which gives this fantastic camouflage effect. Think of those lazy autumn days kicking leaves and climbing trees, tadpole collecting, and throwing sticks into the stream, watching dragon flies flitting from here to there whilst watching the ripples in the pond.

Sizes
6-12 months, (12-24 months, 24-36 months).

Materials
Debbie Bliss Maya, Chunky (100% handspun wool).
6-12 months requires 50 grams.
12-24 months requires 50 grams.
24-36 months requires 100 grams.
5mm needles.

Tension
10cm + 10cm square should have 17 stitches and 25 rows.

Method
Ear flap.
Cast on 3 stitches.
Work in plain knit (garter stitch). Increase at each end of 1 row and alternate rows until 13 (15,15) stitches on needle.
Garter stitch 9 (9,11) rows.
Repeat for 2nd ear flap.

Using the empty needle cast on 7 (8,9) stitches. Knit across 1st ear flap.
Cast on 23 (24, 29) stitches.
Knit across 2nd ear flap. Cast on 7 (8,9) stitches. 63 (70,77) stitches.
Knit 3 rows.

Starting with a knit row and working in stocking stitch, work until work measures 9 (11,13) cms ending with a purl row.

Shape crown
(Knit 5, knit 2 together) repeat to end of row.
Purl 1 row.
(Knit 4, knit 2 together) repeat to end of row.
Purl 1 row.
(Knit 3, knit 2 together) repeat to end of row.
Purl 1 row.
(Knit 2, knit 2 together) repeat to end of row.
Purl 1 row.
(Knit 1, knit 2 together) repeat to end of row.
Purl 1 row.
Knit 2 together across row.
Thread wool through remaining stitches, draw up tightly.

Finish by joining side seam using a large sewing needle.

denim
sun hat

We tend to think of knitting things to wear in the winter, things to keep us warm, this hat is definitely for the summer.

I have used Rowan denim for the cream and blue and Jaeger Aqua cotton for the red. Both yarns are cool, in both senses of the word, for the summer. The stripes on the hat give them a nautical feel. Summers on the beach looking out to a life on the ocean waves, cruising around the coast in your own yacht… … or a bit of paddling, beach cricket and then fish and chips sitting on the beach front wall! Either way this is a gorgeous hat for the nautically minded among us.

Sizes
6-12 months, (12-24 months).

Materials
Rowan Denim for cream and blue and Jaeger Aqua cotton for red. Alternatively use 100% cotton 4ply in similar colours.

6-12 months	50 grams of cream
	10 grams of blue
	10 grams of red
12-24 months	100 grams of blue
	10 grams of cream
	10 grams of red

4 mm knitting needles.

Tension
10cm + 10cm square should have 20 stitches and 26 rows.

Method
Starting at the crown
Cast on 6 stitches in cream (blue).
Knit 1 stitch, increase one stitch knitwise into every stitch to end of row (11 stitches).
Purl 1 row.
Knit 1, increase 1 stitch into every alternate stitch to end of row. Knit 1 (16 stitches).
Knit 1, increase 1 stitch into every alternate stitch to last 2 stitches. Knit 2. (23 stitches).
Purl 1 row.
Knit 1, increase 1 stitch into every alternate stitch to end of row (34 stitches).
Purl 1 row.
Knit 1, increase 1 stitch into every alternate stitch to last 2 stitches. Knit 2. (50 stitches).
Purl 1 row.

Small size only - *(Knit 2, increase 1 stitch). Repeat from * until last 2 stitches. Knit 2. (66 stitches).

Large size only - Knit 1, increase 1 stitch into every alternate stitch to last 2 stitches. Knit 2. (74 stitches).
Purl 1 row.
Stocking stitch 16 (26) rows.

Stripes
Change colour to Red (Red) work 2 rows.
Change colour to Blue (Cream) work 2 rows.
Change colour to Cream (Blue) work 2 rows.
Change colour to Blue (Cream) work 2 rows.
Change colour to Red (Red) work 2 rows.
Change colour back to main Cream (Blue).
(Knit 5 stitches, increase into next stitch) repeat to end of row. *Large size* repeat to last 2 stitches. Knit 2. 77 (86) stitches.
Purl 1 row.
(Knit 6, increase into next stitch) repeat to end of row. *Large size* repeat to last 2 stitches. Knit 2. 88 (98) stitches.
Purl 1 row.
(Knit 7, increase into next stitch) repeat to end of row. *Large size* repeat to last 2 stitches. Knit 2. 99 (110) stitches.

Small size only
(Purl 8, increase into next stitch) repeat to end of row. (110 stitches).
(Knit 9, increase into next stitch) repeat to end of row. (121 stitches).
(Purl 10, increase into next stitch) repeat to end of row. (132 stitches).
Knit 1 row.
Purl 1 row.
Cast off loosely.

Large size only
Purl 1 row.
(Knit 8, increase into next stitch), repeat to last 2 stitches. Knit 2. (122 stitches).
Purl 2, increase into next stitch purlwise.
(Purl 9 stitches, increase 1 stitch) repeat to end of row. (134 stitches).
(Knit 10 stitches, increase into next stitch) repeat to last 2 stitches, knit 2. (146 stitches).
Purl 2, (increase into next stitch, purl 11) repeat to end of row. (158 stitches).
Knit 1 row.
Purl 1 row.
Cast off loosely.
Sew up side seam with matching yarn colours.

ear flap hat

I was trying to think of a different way to describe this
hat, but as all the others are exactly as described I
stuck with 'ear flap hat'. And despite it's name this
stripy 'ear flap hat' is probably my favourite of all.

By using Rowan Calmer it is so very, very soft
and looks absolutely delightful when worn.
It uses the stocking stitch and purl stitch and is again
a very simple hat to knit, which makes a beautiful gift.

Sizes
Newborn, (6-12 months, 12-24 months).

Materials
Rowan Calmer.
Newborn, 50 grams - 25 grams of each colour for stripes.
6-12 months, 50 grams - 25 grams of each colour.
12-24 months, 100 grams - 50 grams of each colour.
4.5mm knitting needles.

Tension
10cm + 10cm square should have 23 stitches and 34 rows.

Method
Cast on 11 stitches for all sizes (starting at the crown).
Knit 1, increase in every stitch to end of row. (21 stitches). Purl 1 row.
Change colour. Increase in 1st stitch, (knit 1, increase 1) repeat to end of row. (32 stitches).
Purl 1 row.
Change colour. Increase in 1st stitch, (knit 2, increase 1) repeat to last stitch, knit 1.
(43 stitches).
Purl 1 row.
Change colour. Increase on 1st stitch, (knit 3, increase 1) repeat to end of row.
(54 stitches).
Purl 1 row.
Change colour. Increase on 1st stitch, (knit 4, increase 1) repeat to end of row.
(65 stitches).
Purl 1 row.
Change colour. Increase on 1st stitch, (knit 5, increase 1) repeat to end of row.
(76 stitches).
Purl 1 row.
Change colour. Increase on 1st stitch, (knit 6, increase 1) repeat to end of row.
(87 stitches).
Purl 1 row. Newborn size crown is complete.

2nd and 3rd sizes only:
Change colour. Increase on 1st stitch, (knit 7, increase 1) repeat to end of row.
(98 stitches).
Purl 1 row. 6-12 month crown is complete.

3rd size only.
Change colour. Increase on 1st stitch, (knit 8, increase 1) repeat to end of row.
(109 stitches).
Purl 1 row.
Continue in stocking-stitch for 27 (35,43) rows finishing on a knit row.
Remember to change colours for stripes.
Cast off 10 (11,13) purlwise. Purl 12 (17,19). Cast off 43 (42,45) purlwise.
Purl 12 (17,19). Cast off 10 (11,13) purlwise.
Rejoin wool to first lot of stitches, work 2 rows.
Knit 2 together on each end on alternate rows until 2 (3,3) stitches remain.
Purl 2 (3,3) together. Slip remaining stitches onto a medium crochet
hook and work chain until required length. Repeat for other ear flap.
Finish by joining side seam using matching wool and a large sewing needle.

The things which the child loves remain in the domain of the heart until old age. The most beautiful thing in life is that our souls remain over the places where we once enjoyed ourselves

pom pom hat

This is an old favourite, the traditional pom pom hat which we never tire of. The colours, (muted greens, blues and reds) and wool I have chosen, give this a contemporary and modern twist. Again think surfer dude rather than trainspotter. The wool is Debbie Bliss Cashmerino Aran DK, lovely and soft, yet perfect to keep you warm on a cold winters day.

This hat always works well with a matching scarf, so I have given instructions to make a quick scarf. I love the pom-pom, but you can leave this to be a pom-pom-less hat if you like.

Sizes
6-12 months, (12-24 months, 24-36 months).

Materials
Debbie Bliss Cashmerino Aran DK.
6-12 months and 12-24 months require 50 grams made up of 5 different colours.
24-36 months requires 100 grams made up from 5 different colours.
4mm needles.

Tension
10cm + 10cm square should have 26 stitches and 29 rows in unstretched fabric.

Method
Cast on 82 (102,122) stitches in first chosen colour. Working in knit 2, purl 2 rib work 6 rows, then change colour.
Repeat this until the work measures 17 (19, 21) cm from the beginning.
End after the third row in the stripe.
Shape top.
(Purl 2, knit 2 together) repeat to last 2 stitches. Purl 2.
(Knit 2 together, purl 1) repeat to last 2 stitches. Knit 2 together.
Purl 2 together across row until last stitch. Purl 1.
Knit 2 together across row until last stitch. Knit 1.
Thread wool through remaining stitches, draw up tightly and fasten securely.

Join side seam using matching threads and a large sewing needle.

Make and attach a Pom Pom if desired.

Scarf
Using 4mm needles cast on 42 stitches in chosen colour and work 20 rows in knit 2, purl 2 rib.
Work 6 rows of each colour.
Change back to 1st colour and continue until scarf measures approx 50cm.
Work another 6 rows of each colour then 20 rows of main 1st colour.
Cast off.

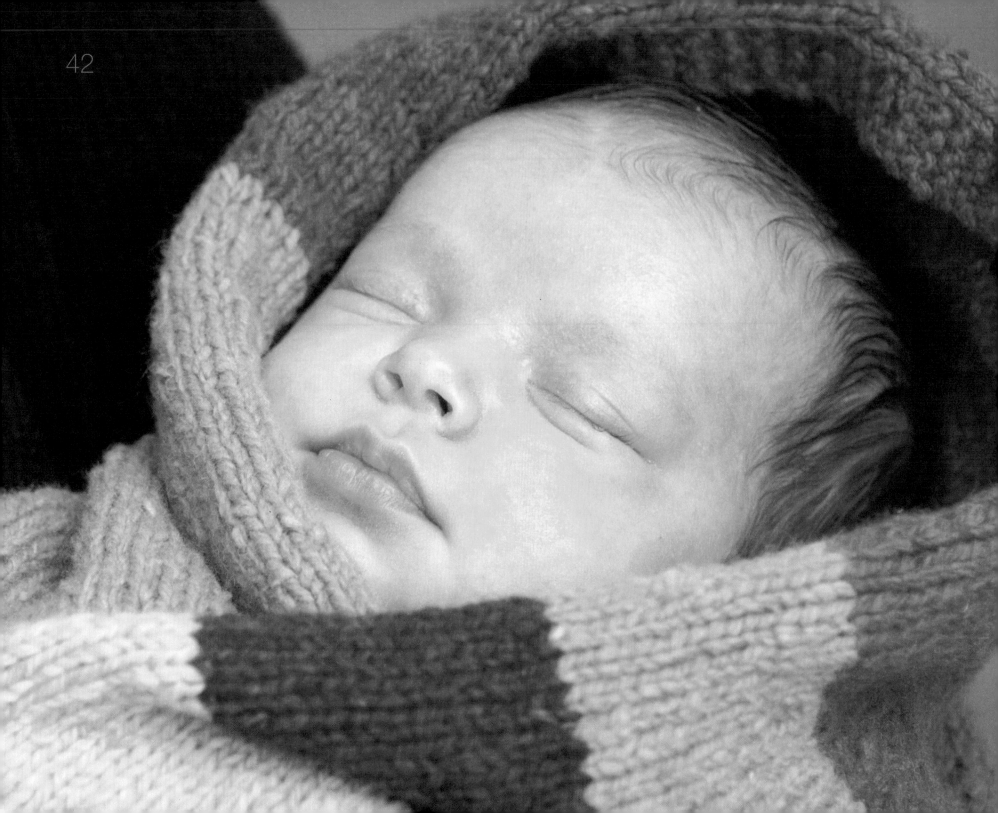

scarf hat

The pom pom hat looks great matched with a scarf and now here is a hat, which is a scarf, or perhaps it is a scarf, which is a hat. Either way it is a great idea, especially for newborns.

The wool is Rowan Yorkshire Tweed and the colours are fantastic autumn swatches of purples, greens, reds and pink. Really subtle yet distinct, a way of making a statement without having to shout about it.

This scarf hat, which is loose fitting, still reminds me of babies that are tightly swaddled and strapped close to their mothers. Any baby will sleep well with this beautiful design wrapped around them.

Sizes
Newborn, (6-12 months)

Materials
Rowan Yorkshire Tweed DK.
Small size requires 150grams, made up of:
50 grams purple (A)
50 grams pale green (B)
50 grams red (C)
50 grams pink (D)

Large size requires 300 grams, made up of:
100 grams purple (A)
100 grams pale green (B)
50 grams red (C)
50 grams pink (D)
4mm knitting needles.

Tension
10cm + 10cm square should have 20 stitches and 31 rows.

Method
Cast on 40 (50) stitches in colour A.
Knit 8 rows in plain knit.
Next row-knit 4 stitches, purl to last 4 stitches, knit 4 stitches.
Next row-knit.
Next row-knit 4 stitches, purl to last 4 stitches, knit 4 stitches.
Next row-knit.
Repeat the last 4 rows until work measures 7cm (8.5cm).
Keep the same stitch pattern across the row, and change colour only on knit rows, continue:
change to colour (B) work another 7cm (8.5cm)
change to colour (C) work another 7cm (8.5cm)
change to colour (D) work another 7cm (8.5cm)
change colour back to (A) work another 7cm (8.5cm)
change colour to (B) work another 7cm (8.5cm)
change colour to (C) work another 7cm (8.5cm)
change colour to (D) work 15cm (18cm)
change to colour (C) work for 30cm (35cm)
change to colour (A) for 3cms
work 4 rows in plain knit (garter stitch)
change to colour (B) and work 4 rows in plain knit. Cast off.

Making up
Fold the scarf in half lengthwise. On one side, join the seam from the fold down for 17cms using a matching yarn and a large sewing needle.

square hat

This is the easiest of all the hats, is great fun and can be made with or without the tassles. I have gone for deep purples and reds, but you can experiment with all sorts of colours. This hat would also look great with a motif on the front, which as you become more experienced you will be able to design and add yourself.

The yarn is Rowan Cashsoft 4ply, which is exactly as it says, soft. This hat is ideal if you are in a REAL hurry to find a present, as you will be able to finish it in a flash.

Sizes
Newborn, (6-12 months, 12-24 months).

Materials
Rowan Cashsoft 4 ply.
3mm knitting needles.

Tension
10cm + 10cm square should have 28 stitches and 39 rows.

Method
Back-Cast on 40 (50,60) stitches.
Work 6 (10,10) rows in knit 1, purl 1 rib.
(You can use garter or stocking stitch here if preferred).
Work in stocking stitch until work measures 11cm (15,19cm).
Cast off loosely.

Front-Repeat as back.

Sew up top seam, then side seams.

If desired make two tassels in a contrasting colour and sew onto top corners of hat.

Making Tassels
Cut a piece of stiff card 10cm x 20cm. Wrap wool around the 10cm width 20 times. Pass another piece of wool around the wrapped wool going between the wool and card, pull all the strands together by tying a knot. Turn the card over and cut the bundle of strands on the other side of the card exactly opposite the knot, remove the card. This gives you a loose tassle. Fold the strands using the tie as a mid point and bind the strands together near the tie. Trim the tassle ends to give a neat edge and attach to hat using a matching thread, and a large sewing needle.

Children have neither past nor future;
they enjoy the present, which very
few of us do

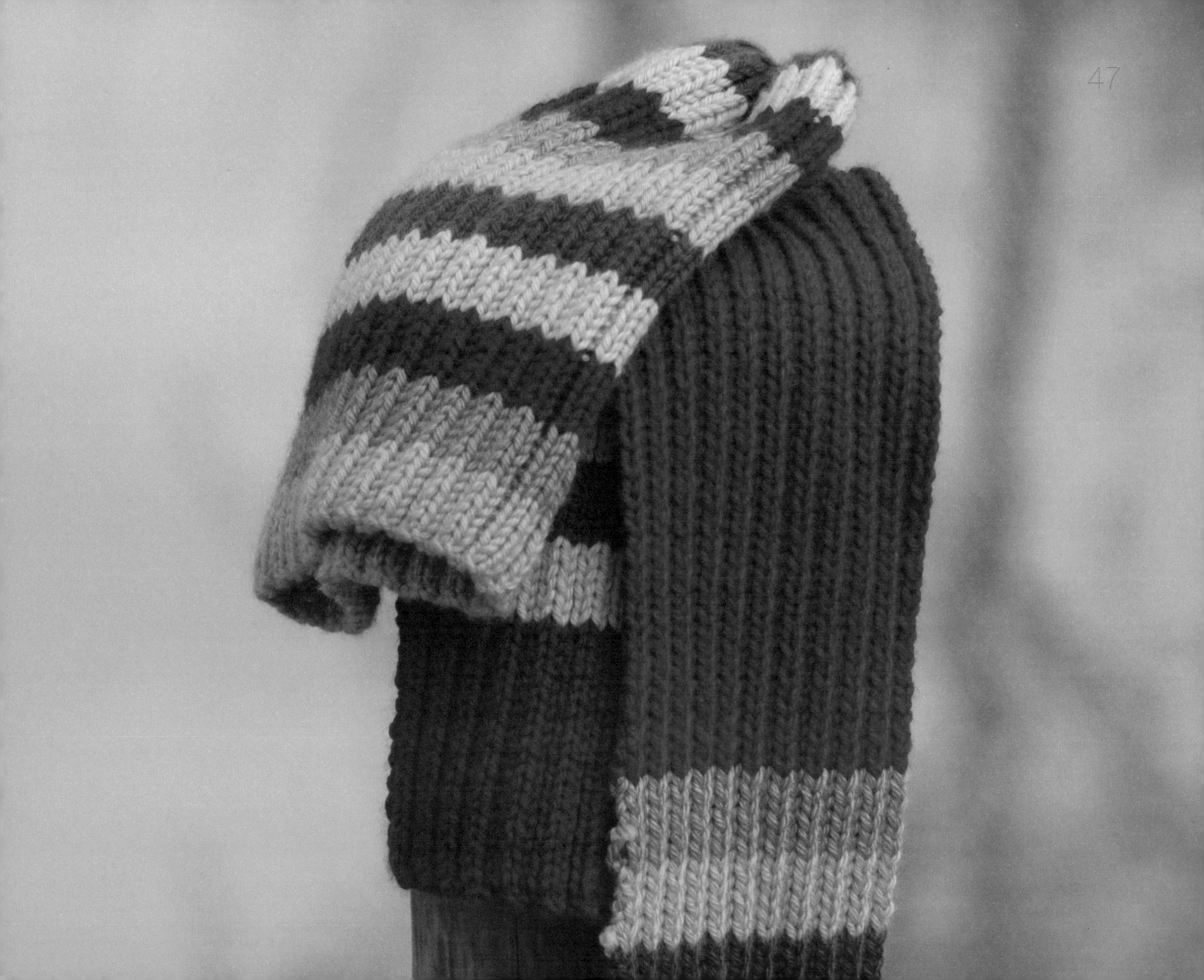

wrapping your handknitted gifts...

After creating this wonderful knitted hat, it is always nice to wrap it in a personal way, so that the recipient knows they are getting something special. There are many ways to do this, some elaborate and complicated and some simple. As this book is all about 'ease', here are three simple ideas to get you going.

Tissue Paper.

Tissue paper is one of the simplest ways to wrap your gift and one of the nicest. Try and choose a colour that complements your gift and if the paper gets a bit wrinkled and crinkly don't worry as this often adds to the charm. By tying the package with a bit of leftover yarn and adding a gift tag with the recipients name on, your gift will look great.

Boxes and bags.

You can buy boxes and bags in all sorts of shapes and sizes from stationery and craft supply stores. You could either place your gift straight into the box or bag with a few bits of shredded tissue paper or if you have wrapped the gift, place that into the box. The recipient will then have a nice box to store things, as well as your gift.

As you can see these simple ideas will make your knitted gift that extra bit special.

knitting abbreviations...

Whilst we have spelt out all the knitting instructions in this book, most patterns that are available tend to use abbreviations.

With this in mind I thought it would be useful to list the more commonly used abbreviations to help you on any future projects you may undertake.

alt	=	alternate
beg	=	beginning
cm	=	centimetre(s)
cont	=	continue
dec	=	decrease
foll	=	following
in	=	inch(es)
inc	=	increase one stitch by working into front and back of stitch
K(k)	=	knit
kfb	=	knit into front and back of stitch
m1	=	make one stitch
mm	=	millimetres
patt	=	pattern
P(p)	=	purl
rem	=	remaining
rep	=	repeat
st(s)	=	stitch(es)
skpo	=	slip 1, knit1, pass slipped stitch over
sl	=	slip
st st	=	stocking stitch
tbl	=	through back loop
tog	=	together
yf	=	yarn forward
yon	=	yarn over needle
yrn	=	yarn round needle

further help...

I have listed a few websites where you can buy wool and accessories on-line. I have also found these sites great fun to browse through and get inspiration. Happy surfing...

www.loop.gb.com

Loop is a shop in North London which has a fantastic selection of knitting yarns and accessories sourced from all over the world. Loop is a knitters heaven with plenty to give you lots of inspiration... everything to do with all things knitting.

www.angelyarns.com

Angel Yarns is an online store stocking a wide range of speciality knitting yarns, knitting books, patterns and accessories. Definitely worth a browse.

www.laughinghens.com

Laughinghens.com is a great online one-stop shop for quality wools designs and great ideas. They stock some wonderful knitting needles and their kits are worth looking at.

www.knitrowan.com

The website that stocks all things Rowan, from books and patterns to yarn and accessories. There are also details for events and workshops, so definitely worth keeping an eye on.

acknowledgements...

Pattern checker: **Hannah Greenaway**
Knitters: **Jean Studholme, Christine Hart**

With thanks to:
**My supportive husband
(and wonderful photographer) Richard Bailey,
my good friend and creative genius Steve Gardiner,
my children Billie-Jo, Daniel and Cydney.**

Contact: **fiona@fionabaileydesigns.com**
Contact the publishers: **info@baileyhartpublishing.com**

It was one of those perfect English autumnal days which occur more frequently in memory than in life.